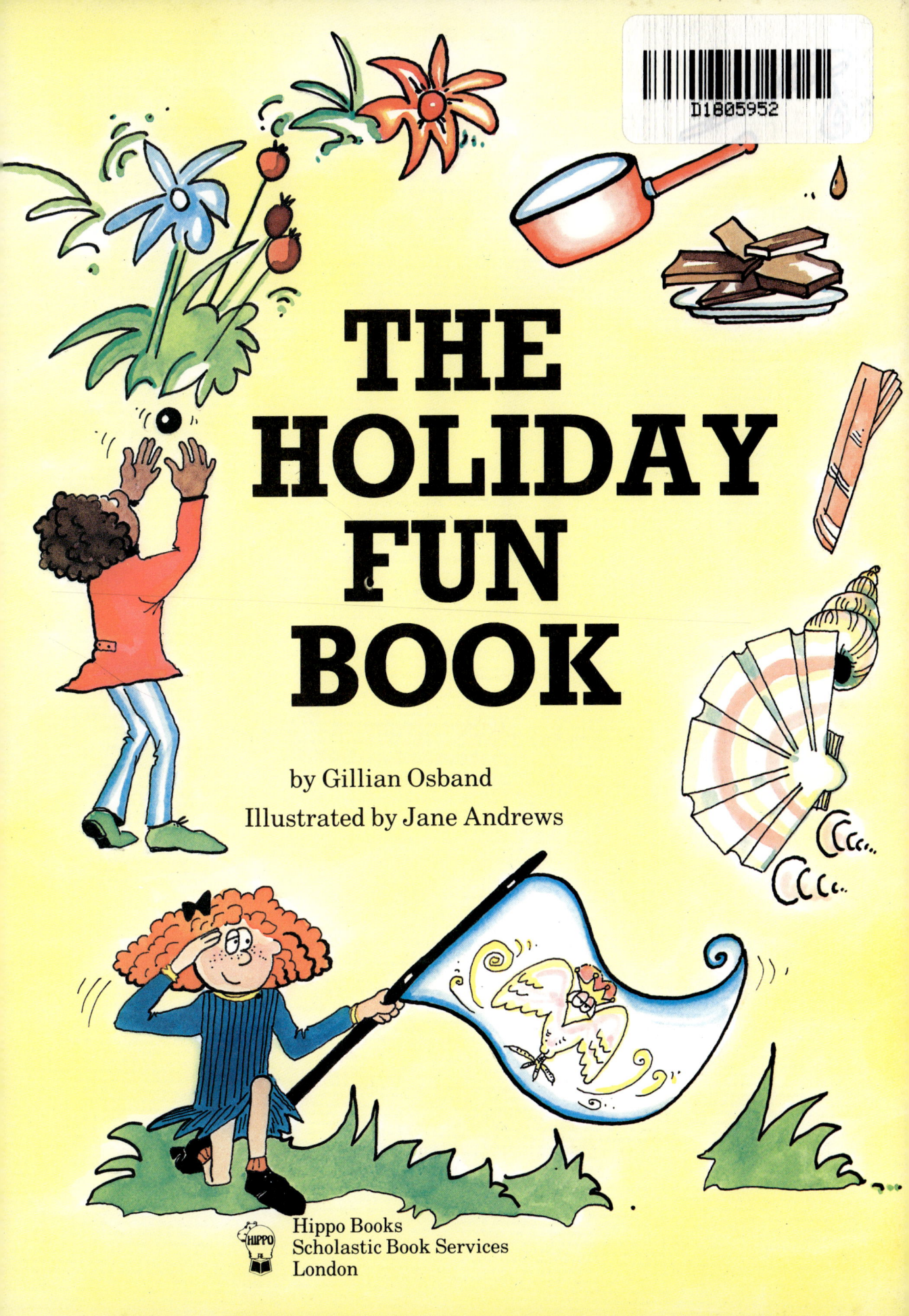

THE HOLIDAY FUN BOOK

by Gillian Osband

Illustrated by Jane Andrews

Hippo Books
Scholastic Book Services
London

D1805952

Scholastic Book Services
10 Earlham Street, London WC2 9LN, England

Scholastic Books Services
730 Broadway, New York, NY 10003, USA

Scholastic Tab Publications Ltd
123 Newkirk Road, Richmond Hill,
Ontario L4C 3G5, Canada

Ashton Scholastic, Box 579, Gosford
New South Wales, Australia

Ashton Scholastic Ltd., 165 Marua Road,
Panmure, Auckland, New Zealand

The Holiday Fun Book
First Published in the UK
by Scholastic Publications Ltd., 1985

The Holiday Fun Text
© Manor Lodge Productions Ltd., 1985
Holiday Fun Book Illustrations © Jane Andrews
1985
Did I Ever Tell You ... About Being Banned For Life
From The Boating Pool © Iris Grender 1983
from Did I Ever Tell You ... About My Birthday Party
by Iris Grender published by Hutchinson.
Super Gran and The Match © Forrest Wilson 1984
from The Television Adventures of Super Gran by
Forrest Wilson published by Puffin Books
Super Gran and The Match Illustrations
© David McKee 1984
Toad's Road Game © Judy Brook 1984
from The Wind in the Willows Activity Book
published by Andre Deutsch
Postman Pat Illustrations
© Celia Berridge and Ivor Wood 1982
taken from the Postman Pat Books
published by Andre Deutsch.

All Rights Reserved

Printed in Spain by Mateu Cromo, Madrid

CONTENTS

GAMES, GAMES, GAMES ... For Out Of Doors.

FLY (any number)

You Need: 6 sticks.

How To Play:

Place the sticks about 30cm apart.

Each player has to jump over each stick **without touching it** and **without jumping over a space between two sticks.**

The last jumper takes a long jump over the last stick and calls out the number of one of the sticks, for example, stick 3. The third stick is then placed where the jumper has jumped to – making a bigger space to jump between sticks 2 and 4, and another bigger space to jump at the end.

The game goes on until the spaces between the sticks get so big that no-one can jump them. The person to jump furthest is the last jumper next time.

Remember: only one jump is allowed between sticks.

Did You Know? *The British Museum in London has footballs once owned and used by the Pharoahs of Ancient Egypt.*

Did You Know? *In the Ancient Olympic Games only two running sprints were included, and false starts were punished by whipping.*

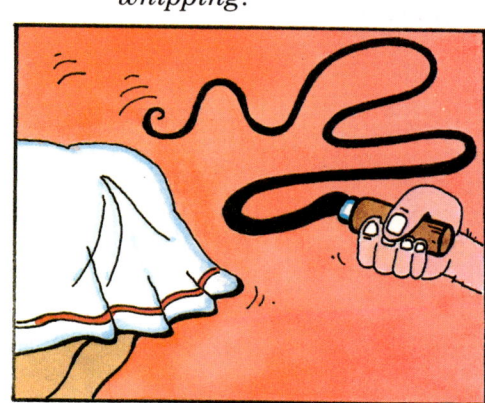

SQUIRTS

(2 or more players)

WARNING: This is a very wet and messy game!

You Need: An empty plastic bottle (detergent ones are good) for each player – all about the same size; water!

How to Play:

SQUIRTS can either be a free-for-all, or you can divide into two teams with one team tying string around their waists.

Fill the bottles up with water. When everyone has a full bottle – squirt the water at each other, or the opposite team. If you are hit – you're **OUT**. Whoever stays driest longest – **WINS....**

OUT!

CRAZY RACES

WALKING BACKWARDS

Anyone can walk forwards – so this race is walking **BACKWARDS – it's YSAE!**

Mark out your course – you can include obstacles to go around – and off you back!

Did You Know? *An American, Plennie L. Wingo, left California, U.S.A., on April 15th 1931, and* **walked backwards** *to Istanbul, Turkey. He didn't get there until October 24th 1932!*

Why are mosquitoes religious?

First they sing then they prey on you!

What did the earwig say when it fell off the wall?

'Ere we go!

Knock, knock.
Who's there?
You..
You who?
You who! Is there anybody in?

CAN IT!

You Need: 2 large cans (juice, soup etc.) for each racer. The cans need to have been pierced open, not had the tops removed. (You can also use empty paint cans with the lid on.)

Mark out the race course which should be about 8 giant steps long.

WARNING: you are not allowed to put your feet on the ground. How do you race across the course? .... On the cans!!!

How Do You Do It?

1. Hold one can. Put the other can on the ground just behind the starting line. Step onto the can – and balance. You may be able to get both feet on it.

2. When everyone is balanced – the Starter says **'GO!'**

3. Put the can you've been holding on the ground in front of you. Step onto it. Pick up the first can and place it in front of you – and step onto that one! Keep going like this until you have crossed the line.

Looks easy – but it isn't!!!
If you over-balance and fall off your stepping-tin – back to the beginning you go....

CATCH IT IF YOU CAN

You can play this on your own – or take it in turns and see who drops the ball first, and who can achieve the most throws.

You need to go through at least 6 different throws. Here are some ideas, but you can make up some of your own or add some more difficult ones at the end.

You Need: A ball; a wall.

How To Play Catch It If You Can:

Stand about 2 metres away from the wall and try these different throws.

1. Throw the ball, let it bounce once, catch it in you left hand.

2. Throw, catch it in your right hand (no bounce).

3. Throw, clap twice, catch the ball with both hands.

4. Throw, clap hands in front and behind, catch the ball.

5. Balance on one leg, throw and catch.

6. Throw, spin right round, catch the ball.

SCAVENGER HUNT

There's nothing like a good scavenge! Take it in turns to make up a list of things to hunt for. Here is one to start you off:

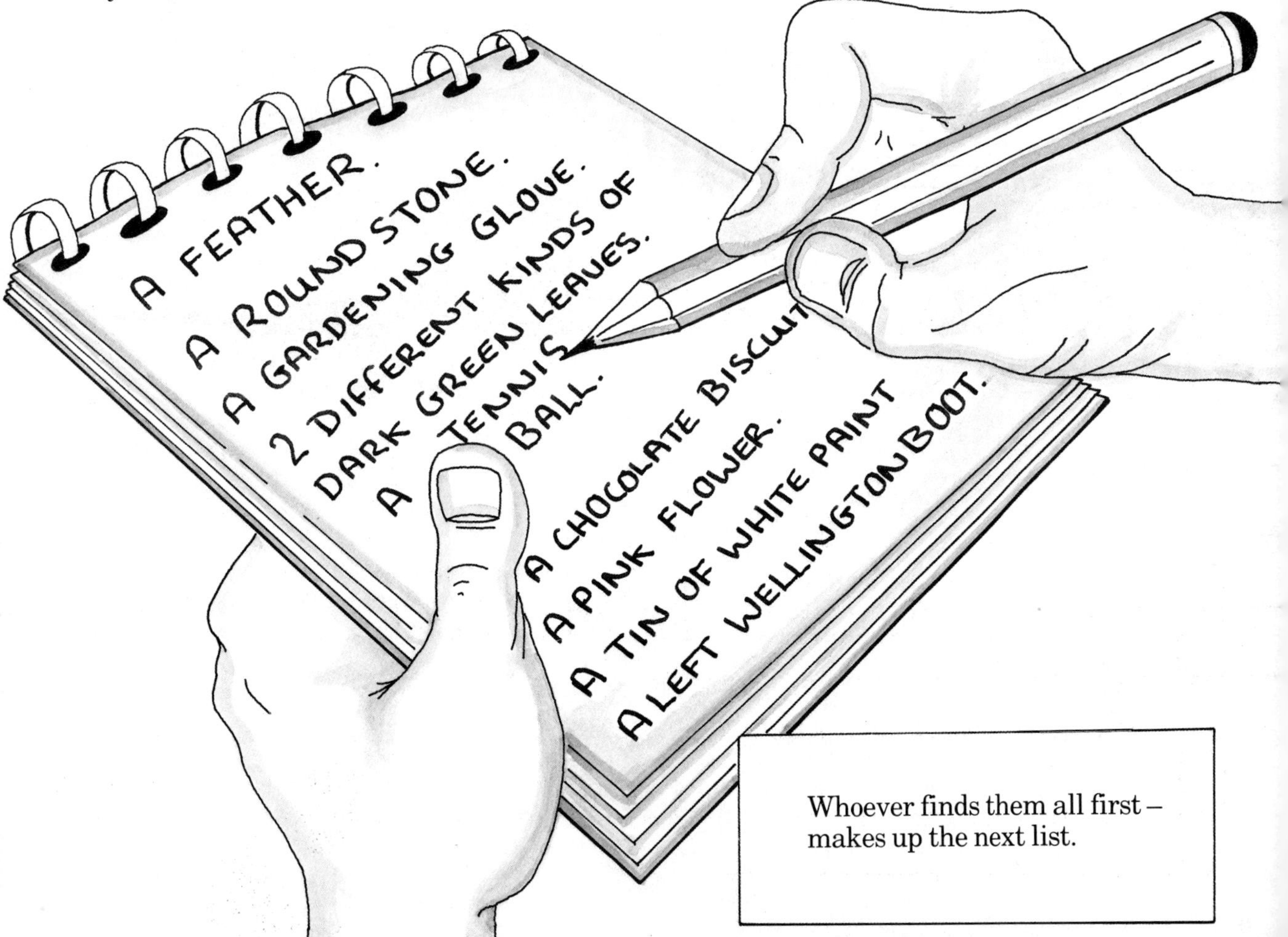

A FEATHER.
A ROUND STONE.
A GARDENING GLOVE.
2 DIFFERENT KINDS OF DARK GREEN LEAVES.
A TENNIS BALL.
A CHOCOLATE BISCUIT
A PINK FLOWER.
A TIN OF WHITE PAINT
A LEFT WELLINGTON BOOT.

Whoever finds them all first – makes up the next list.

SUPER GRAN AND THE MATCH Forrest Wilson

Super Gran zoomed through the Chisleton streets on roller skates delivering Meals On Wheels to the town's old folks. Only she was doing it too dangerously for PC Leekie, who was on point duty at the time. One minute he was standing there directing traffic, and the next he was flat on his back with plates of stew showering down on him!

The trouble was that she had let her attention wander to a poster on a hoarding she was passing. It read: FA CUP. SATURDAY 4TH. CHISLETON ATHLETIC V. ROYSTOWN ROVERS.

As Leekie struggled to his feet, wiping pieces of potato off his uniform, Super Gran apologized. 'Jings! I'm awful sorry – I wasn't looking where I was going and I was reading that poster. Imagine the Rovers coming to play here in Chisleton! Willard's all excited about it.'

'Well, I shouldn't get too excited,' Leekie advised, as he removed a piece of carrot from his ear. 'It'll be a walk-over for the Rovers.'

'Och well, we'll all be there anyway to cheer them on. Won't you?'

'I'll be there, all right, on crowd control,' Leekie said. 'That is, if I manage to get all this stew out of my uniform before then! Humph!'

Meanwhile, the Scunner was also in a stew!

He was standing in his lounge reading a letter he had just received.

'Listen to this, Tub: "Dear Scunner, unless you pay me the two thousands pounds you owe, all your rotten, decayed, hollow teeth will be rattling about

in your rotten, decayed, hollow head. Yours affectionately, Vincent Ruff." What do you think of that, Tub?'

'M'mmm,' said Tub thoughtfully. 'He writes a nice letter, doesn't he?'

'What! A nice letter? You fat baboon! The point is, I don't have the money to pay him.'

'Then how are we going to eat – without money?' a worried Tub asked, thinking only of his stomach.

'And how am I going to eat without teeth?' the worried Scunner retorted, thinking only of his mouth.

He looked even more worried as the letter continued: ' "PS: I'll personally collect the two grand on Saturday, after the match." '

'Match? What match?' the Scunner asked.

'The cup-tie between Athletic and the Roystown Rovers,' Tub explained. 'Mr Ruff is the Rovers' chairman.'

'Yeeks! Saturday!' the Scunner yelled, shuddering. 'But that's tomorrow! We haven't much time!' He closed his mouth, as if to protect his teeth from Vincent Ruff's rough hands!

'Yeah, I know,' Tub sympathized. 'Athletic have a rotten team. They'll never be ready in time . . .'

'I'm not bothered about them!' the Scunner yelled. 'I'm bothered about me and my teeth! I'm rather attached to them!'

He snapped his fingers. 'I've an idea. Athletic haven't a chance, you say? Then supposing I put a bet on them – to win . . . ?'

'What?' Tub was flabbergasted. 'A bookie would give you a thousand to one against them winning . . .'

'That's what I mean,' the Scunner said, smiling. 'All I need to put on is two pounds and I'll win two thousand. The two thousand I need to pay off Vincent.'

'But Uncle, they can't win! They never win! If they even win a throw-in, during a game, they do a lap of honour!'

'Don't worry, I told you – I've got an idea. See these?' He pulled two moth-eaten pounds-notes from his wallet and waved them in Tub's face. 'I'm going to bet on Chisleton to win this cup-tie, at a thousand to one.'

Tub was appalled at his uncle's stupidity. For apart from the two pound-notes, the Scunner was broke!

Meanwhile Super Gran and Willard, like everyone else in town, were excited about the mighty Rovers, the best team in England, visiting little, lowly, non-League Chisleton.

But Mr Small, Athletic's manager, didn't share everyone's excitement. For his team was unfit, shabbily dressed and badly trained. And no one could remember when they last drew a match, never mind winning!

'Look at them,' he sighed. 'We're the laughing-stock of our non-League league!'

Super Gran and Willard were watching them training at their dilapidated stadium when Mr Small emerged from his office on to the pitch.

'Och, away with you,' Super Gran said, trying to cheer him up. 'I'm sure Athletic will play their best.'

'Athletic? Humph!' he snorted. 'the only thing that's "athletic" about them is their name! The players aren't athletic! Just look at them . . .!'

Super Gran and Willard had to admit that this was possibly the worst team in the whole of England! In Britain, even!

'And what makes it worse,' he went on gloomily, 'is that the Rovers have the best striker in England. Gary Bootle. So we'll be up against him.'

'And all we've got is Norman Earnmore,' Willard pointed out. 'Our star striker.'

'Yeah!' mutterd Mr Small gloomily. 'And he's long past his best. The Rovers'll slaughter us!'

'It's a pity I can't play for you, isn't it?' Super Gran said.

'I only wish you could, Super Gran,' he sighed. 'Maybe then it would be more of a game.'

'Oh . . . er . . . well . . . you see . . .' begun the Scunner, taken aback.

'Oh, that's jolly nice of you,' Mr Small smiled, and left the Rover's dressing-room to return to his own, leaving behind a stunned Scunner.

'Thanks, boss,' said Norman Earnmore, presently, taking a glass. 'But aren't you having any?'

'No thanks, lad. I only drink champagne after we win a match. So I never get the chance to drink the stuff, do I?'

It took the dazed Scunner a few minutes to think of an excuse for visiting the Athletic dressing-room. and by the time he did so, the champagne had been scoffed!

'Let me wish you all the best . . .' he began, then spotted the empty glasses. He was too late.

'You'll never win that bet now,' Tub said, as the Scunner, shocked to the core, staggered out into the tunnel. He looked deadly pale at the thought of what Vincent Ruff's ruffians would do to him – and to his precious teeth!

'Help! I'm off!' he yelled, and ran towards the exit.

But someone was blocking his way. 'Going somewhere, Scunner?' It was Vincent.

'Er . . . yes . . . no . . . that is . . . I'm going to my seat in the stand . . .'

'Then you're going the wrong way, aren't you?' Vincent smiled, evilly. 'The stand is that way . . .' He pointed in the opposite direction and ushered the Scunner and Tub forward. 'And I'll see you later, with your – or rather, my – two thousand quid.'

The Scunner was sure that Vincent must have known what he was up to with the champagne. For he was singing a song as he forced them towards the stand and the words were: 'Have a drink, have a drink, have a drink on me . . .'

Presently the golden-haired golden boy of English soccer, Gary Bootle, led his wealthy, well-dressed, star teammates out on to the pitch, to the tumultuous cheers of their thousands of supporters. Vincent followed them, his raincoat draped over his shoulders like a cloak, his clasped hands held aloft like a champion boxer. And their supporters cheered louder than ever.

Then Norman Earnmore led out his lowly, shuffling, down-at-heel, non-athletic Athletic team-mates to join the Rovers on the field, to a few rather pathetic cheers from Willard, Edison, Super Gran, Leekie and a handful of others – and a lot of boos and cat-calls from the Rovers' support. Then Mr Small joined them and the boos got louder, with cries of 'Get off! Geroutovit . . .!'

Mr Small and Vincent left the pitch and the game started.

At the kick-off Norman Earnmore, by some miracle, got the ball. He dribbled through the Rovers' defence, reached the penalty area and had only the goalkeeper to beat.

But suddenly he spun round on the spot and fell to the ground – fast asleep! The doped champagne was having its effects!

'What on earth's the wee bachle playing at?' Super Gran said from her seat in the stand.

'Well, it's not football, that's for sure,' Willard replied.

'Look! There goes another one!' Edison cried. 'And another . . . and another . . .!'

The whole of the Athletic team fell to the ground and the only sound to be heard in the speechless, now-silent stadium was their loud snores.

'I know Athletic aren't athletic, but that's ridiculous!' an astonished Super Gran said.

'I'll bet they've never actually fallen asleep during a match before, have they?' Edison added.

But worse was to come!

In the brief moments of playing time – between the players falling asleep and being carried off the field by the trainers – Gary Bootle scored seven goals for the Rovers!

Then the referee stopped the match while a discussion took place in the centre of the pitch.

The Rovers players stood around while the two managements met the referee to decide what should be done about the situation. Never before had an entire team fallen asleep on the pitch during an FA cup-tie!

'There's nothing else for it,' the referee said, 'I'll have to abandon the match. The rules say . . .'

'But the rules don't cover this situation,' Mr Small pointed out. 'It wasn't foreseen that this would ever happen.'

'Nevertheless,' the referee went on, 'there is no alternative. You're seven goals down, your reserve team is playing away from home – and you've no one left to continue the match.'

'But if I got another team together? Mr Small pleaded. 'Couldn't we continue then?'

'We-ell, it's not strictly legal,' the referee told him, 'but – oh, what difference will it make?'

Athletic had no chance before the start of the match, and they had even less of a chance now. No team and seven goals down! What harm could it do, the referee thought. And besides, the crowd had come to see a match – the Rovers supporters had travelled hundreds of miles – so why shouldn't it continue, if Athletic could find a replacement team?

'Oh, go on then,' he relented. 'If you can scrape up a team I'll re-start the match.'

So Mr Small put a call out on the stadium's loudspeaker: 'Anyone willing to take part in this match against the Rovers should report to the dressing-room right away . . .'

Meanwhile Vincent was talking to Gary Bootle about the seven goals he had scored so far!

'We're going to end up in the Guinness Book of Records, my boy! Whoever they field – we'll make mincemeat of them!'

'Yeah,' said Gary, who was not what Super Gran would call a 'blether'!

But neither Vincent nor Gary thought for a moment that a little old lady was about to play against them! For neither of them had ever heard of Super Gran – although they were just about to!

On the pitch, Athletic's non-athletic footballers were puffing and panting and half-heartedly kicking footballs around. Mr Small left them to it and returned to his office.

Meanwhile, the Scunner had decided to have a closer look at the no-chance team he had put his money on. And as there was no way that he and Tub would be invited to watch the team in training, he had to resort to climbing a small hill which overlooked the stadium and using a pair of powerful binoculars!

'See what I mean?' Tub said. 'They're useless, aren't they?'

'Yes, you're right,' the Scunner agreed. 'But luckily I've got a plan to make sure that they do win . . .'

'Win? A plan?' Tub said. 'What is it?'

'I've decided to treat Vincent Ruff to a drink!'

On the Saturday a large, sleek coach stopped outside Athletic's dilapidated stadium. Vincent Ruff, the Rovers' chairman, stepped out of it, followed by their striker, Gary Bootle.

'Phew! It's a bit of a dump, isn't it?' Vincent said. The wealthy, glamorous, mightly Rovers tended to look down their noses at little non-League teams like Chisleton Athletic.

'Yeah,' agreed Gary. He was a man of few words.

Vincent helped his star down the coach steps. 'Be careful, Gary, don't trip. You're worth a million pounds, remember.'

Mr Small emerged from his office to greet the opposition. 'Mr Ruff? Welcome to Chisleton Athletic. I'm Small.'

Yeah, and your team's small and your ground's small and your town's small . . .! thought Vincent, as he looked around the poverty-stricken stadium. The only thing that won't be small today will be our score . . .!

Presently, while the teams were in their dressing-rooms, Super Gran, Willard and Edison stood talking to PC Leekie – on crowd control – near the players' tunnel in the stand.

'This is the big day,' said Leekie, 'when poor little no-chance Athletic face the mighty – wealthy! – Rovers.'

'Yeah,' Willard said. 'Their players earn a fortune every week. And Athletic get practically nothing. It's not fair.'

'Yes,' giggled Edison, 'I'll bet that Norman Earnmore wishes he could earn more!'

'Look!' Willard exclaimed, pointing towards the tunnel. 'The Scunner! What's he doing there?'

They turned just in time to see the Scunner and Tub, carrying a large basket between them, enter one of the dressing-rooms.

'That's funny,' Super Gran said. 'I didn't know the Scunner supported Athletic. It takes him all his time to support himself and Tub!'

'I'll bet they're up to no good,' Edison murmured.

And she was right. For the Scunner was in the Rovers' dressing-room, shaking hands with Vincent Ruff. Or rather, he was having his hand crushed by Vincent's rough grip!

'Well, if it isn't the Scunner,' Vincent greeted him. 'Got my two thousand quid, have you?'

'We-ell, not yet. Not quite. But the matter's in hand.' He grimaced and indicated his damaged digits. 'And speaking of hands, could I have mine back now, please . . ?'

'So – you've put a little bet on Athletic to win, have you?'

'Oh, you've heard?' The Scunner was taken aback.

'I hear everything that goes on!' said Vincent darkly.

The Scunner shook the pain out of his mangled hand and lifted a bottle of champagne and a glass out of the basket. 'No hard feelings about me betting against your team?' he asked.

Vincent shrugged. 'If you want to throw your money away!'

'Well, lets have a drink, shall we?' the Scunner invited.

'Ta! That's very generous of you, isn't it, Gary?'

Gary Bootle, in his strip ready for the match, came over to see what was going on.

'This is Gary Bottle, our star striker . .'

'How d'you do?' said the Scunner, honoured to be introduced to England's biggest and brightest soccer star.

'Yeah,' said Gary, turning away to look for a mirror, to comb his golden locks.

'He doesn't say much,' Vincent explained. 'He says it all with his feet.'

'Just as well, he doesn't say much with his mouth!' the Scunner murmured. 'But you'll all join us in a drink, won't you . . .?'

He turned away to pour the champagne into glasses and secretly slipped some powder into the bottle.

'What're you doing, Uncle?' Tub asked.

'Shhhh! I'm just making sure I win my bet. And making sure that the mighty Rovers bite the dust . .'

He then filled all the glasses which Tub had taken out of the basket, and placed them on a tray.

'The Rovers will get more and more sleepy as the game goes on,' he whispered. 'Dear little Chisleton Athletic will win the tie – and I'll win my bet.'

Tub sniggered. 'I bet you do, Uncle.'

He turned back towards Vincent and his players, with the champagne on the tray. But just as the players' hands reached out to take the glasses, Mr Small entered the dressing-room.

'The best of luck, boys,' he said.

'And the same to you, Mr Small,' Vincent replied, cheerily. 'Here, why don't you take this, as a little gift from our boys to your boys.' And he snatched the tray of drinks from the Scunner and thrust it at Small.

'What? Somebody's granny's gonna play for Athletic?' guffawed Vincent, when he heard the news.

'Ah, but she's Super Gran,' Mr Small explained. 'We only got nine volunteers. So the tenth is a schoolboy and the eleventh is his granny! You don't mind, do you?

'Don't mind? You're joking!' Vincent said. 'The tattier the team the higher the score! Now, let's see, what's the cup record? Wasn't it 26-0 for Preston North End against Hyde, in 1887? We'll easily beat that! In fact, what about the British record? That was 36-0 for Arbroath against Bon Accord, in the Scottish Cup, back in 1885. We could even beat that today!'

Mr Small didn't reply, but his eyes twinkled as he thought of the surprises that were in store for the Rovers when Super Gran got going.

And the surprises started right from the kick-off. For her Super-kick sent the ball the length of the pitch, where it hit the Rovers' keeper and bounced into the net!

The score was 7-1. The fight-back had started!

Meanwhile, the Scunner was as sick as a parrot!

When the Rovers were seven goals up he and Tub had slipped out of the stand, but they were stopped at the exit by two of Vincent's 'heavy mob', who refused to let them leave until the Scunner handed over the two thousand pounds – or his teeth!

'Curses!' he cursed, then: 'More curses! That sounds like another goal. That'll be eight-nothing.'

But as he turned in despair from the exit the news reached him that it was a goal for Chisleton. He brightened. Then he heard that Super Gran had scored it and he brightened even more.

'Good old Super Gran!' he yelled, as he ran towards the stand.

'Where are we going?' asked Tub.

'Back to the game. That sweet, gentle little old lady – that dear old friend of mine – needs all the support she can get . . .'

'Huh? Who?' said Tub, amazed. 'But I thought you hated her!'

By the time they had taken their seats in the stand, Super Gran had scored two more goals.

'Come on . . . Su-per Gran . . .!' the Scunner yelled. 'You show them . . .' Come, on, Ath-letic . . .'

As she dribbled the ball past the Rovers defenders Super Gran glanced at the stand in amazement. She had recognized the voice.

'What's that? The Scunner's on my

side? What's his game, eh?'

She thrust the mystery aside as she passed the ball to Willard, who scored Athletic's fourth goal.

'I never thought it would ever come to this,' the Scunner confessed, embarrassed, 'that I'd cheer on Super Gran!'

'Yeah, but look at her go!' Tub yelled as she weaved her way through the Rovers' defence to score Athletic's fifth goal.

The sixth and seventh goals came soon afterwards, but then there was a lull in the scoring. For the Rovers realized that with the score at seven all they only had to hang on until the final whistle to earn a replay at their own ground. So they brought their entire team back and blocked up the goalmouth to prevent Athletic scoring.

The referee looked at his watch and put his whistle to his lips. Any moment now . . .

In the stand Tub tried to cheer up the Scunner. 'It'll be a draw, so you won't lose your bet . . .'

'Who won't?' the pale-faced Scunner retorted. 'The bet is for Athletic to win – a draw's no use to me!'

'Yeeks! What'll we do, Uncle?' Tub asked.

'What'll we do, Gran?' Willard echoed, as they brought the ball into the Rovers' penalty-box. 'There's not an inch between their players to get the ball through! We've had it . . .!'

'We've had it . . .!' the Scunner echoed, up in the stand. He wrung his hands together and wondered how painful it would be having his teeth knocked out by Vincent's hoodlums!

Meanwhile Vincent, farther along the stand, glanced towards him and smiled. Five seconds more and the Scunner would lose his bet – and his teeth.

But Super Gran, approaching the Rovers' crowded goalmouth, decided that if there was no space for the ball to get through she would have to make some!

She kicked the ball as hard as she could. It hit a defender – and rebounded. The player dropped to his knees, clutching his Super-hit leg, leaving a space where he had been standing for Super Gran's next shot to get through. She hit the rebound as hard as she could and the ball not only entered the net – it went screaming right through it!

'Pheeeep . . .!' The referee's whistle went twice for the goal and for time up.

Chisleton Athletic had done the impossible. They had beaten the mighty Rovers 8-7 and got into the second round of the cup.

But what was more important to the Scunner was that he had won his bet, he could pay off his debt – and he could hang on to his teeth for the time being! From being as sick as a parrot he was now over the moon!

Super Gran led Willard and the makeshift Athletic team in a lap of honour round the pitch, to the cheering of their supporters.

Meanwhile Edison was fighting her way through the cheering, ecstatic crowd to reach the dressing-room, so she could congratulate her friends when they go there. But on the way she passed the Scunner and Tub, who were jumping up and down for joy and hugging each other.

'What's this, Scunner?' she asked. 'You're cheering Athletic's victory? What's the big idea?'

'My dear little prissy missy, this is a happy day in my life. And please pass on my heart-felt congratulations to Super Gran . . .'

'Huh?' Edison didn't know if she was hearing correctly. The Scunner congratulating Super Gran? Was he ill?

'And this is a unique occasion, please note,' he went on. 'For the first time ever, something's happened that's pleased both Super Gran and myself. Super Gran has won a cup-tie and she's saved my precious teeth!

Edison went off towards the dressing-room. She could only shrug, puzzled by the Scunner's strange remarks.

'It's not his teeth, it's his head!' she murmured. 'He's finally gone bananas – he's right round the twist . . .!'

GAMES FOR THE JOURNEY

Here's a **counting out** rhyme to start your game:

Hickerty pickerty i sillickerty
Pompalorum jig,
Every man who has no hair
Generally wears a wig.
One, two, three,
Out goes he!

IN THE GARDEN
(2 or more players)

You wouldn't believe what can happen in the garden! Start the game by saying:

**In the garden there's an
ant acting.**

The next player says: 'In the garden there's a ....' – and ends the sentence with two words beginning with **'B'**. Then the next player ends the sentence with the two words beginning with **'C'**. Take it in turns through the alphabet until one player slips up.

Each player has 3 points. You lose a point if you can't think of anything right away – or if you get it wrong. When you get to **'Z'** start at **'A'** again – but no repeats! Once your 3 points are used up you are out of the game.

FOLLOW MY LEADER
(2 or more players)

You need: pencil and paper for each player.

Pick a leader. Then everyone, except the leader, has to shut their eyes **tight**. The leader then describes a picture – and the players have to draw it **WITHOUT OPENING THEIR EYES!**

SPOT IT!
(1 or more players)

Paper and pencil are useful

One player makes a list of 10 things you have to spot.
For example:
   **a black and white dog
   a pub sign with the word
   'Coach' in it
   a policeman on his motor bike
   a nun
   a BMX being ridden by a girl
   a baby wearing something red
   a video tape shop
   a yellow car (not a van!)
   a lorry with a HAZCHEM
   warning
   a dustcart being loaded.**

Write them down so you don't forget – and the first to spot them all wins and picks the next **10 'Spot Its'!**

TALKING BACKWARDS

One player asks the questions normally – everyone else has to answer talking **BACKWARDS!**

For example:
Question: How many dancing dogs can you see?
Answer: Cat singing a see only can I.

If you make a mistake – you are **TOU!**

CRAZY MEMORY GAME
(2 or more players)

Player 1: Scratches his head once.
Player 2 must: Scratch his head once, then add something himself:
One tap on the nose.
Player 3: Scratches her head once, Tapes her nose once. **AND** ... Coughs three times.

Each player takes it in turn to remember **ALL** the things that have been done before **AND** in the right order – then add his own. One mistake and you are a **DUM-DUM** – and **OUT!**

NAME GAME
(1 or more players)

You Need: Pencil and paper. This is a more difficult game!

Write your name down (or your dog's name, or any name) in a column on the left-hand side of the paper. Then write it in reverse on the right-hand side, like this:

J	**E**
A	**I**
C	**K**
K	**C**
I	**A**
E	**J**

Now – write a message for each letter that starts with the letter on the left – and ends with the letter on the right, like this:

J ump up you	dop **E**
A fter H comes	**I**
C an Donald Duck	quac **K**
K ids love a	picni **C**
I t isn't a lion it's a	pum **A**
E ven I don't know a word ending with a	**J**

Give yourself one minute for each letter of your name – and then try another name.

Why should all men stay away from the letter 'A'?

Because it makes men meAn!

What prize can a cat win?

The A-cat-emy Award!

How does a car go that has a horn, three wheels and no engine?

Beep! Beep!

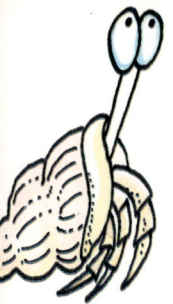

AT THE SEASIDE

There are **101** exciting worlds to explore at the seaside.
EXPLORE!

WARNING:
Rocks are slippery. Pools are often deep.
Find out when the tides go in and out.
Tell someone where you are going.
Never move any animals.
Some fish and jellyfish are poisonous.

Here are a few things to look for:

Flowers and Grasses

SEA BINDWEED

MARRAM GRASS

SEA HOLLY

Seaweeds: found among rocks on the shore-line, or in the sea.

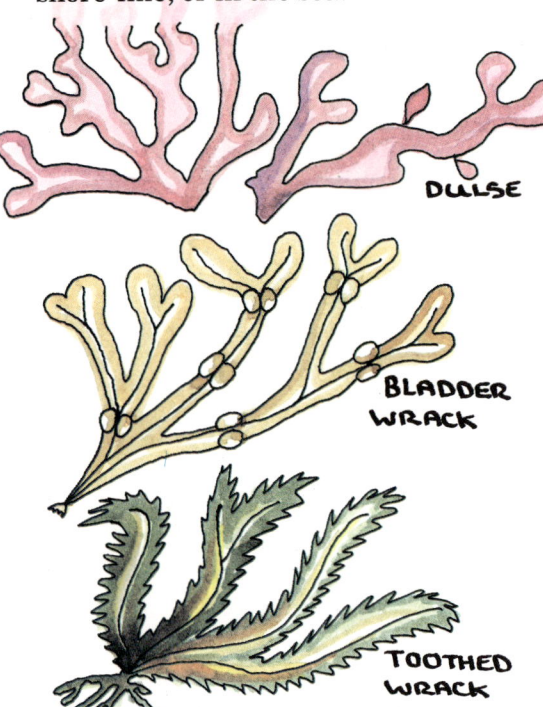

DULSE

BLADDER WRACK

TOOTHED WRACK

Spiny-skinned Animals: look in rock pools.

SEA-URCHIN

COMMON STARFISH

What's black-white, black-white, black-white?

A penguin rolling downhill.

16

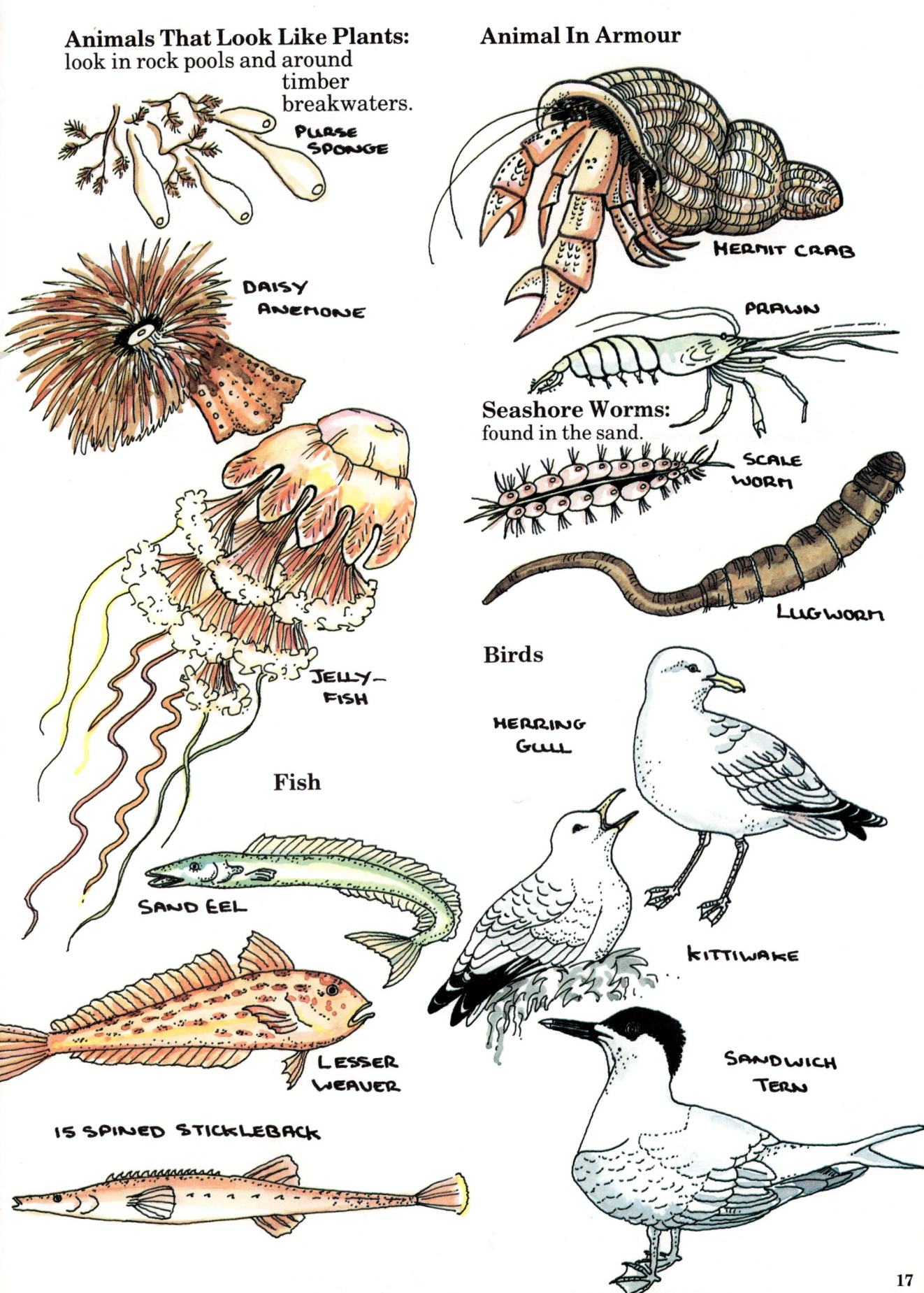

Animals That Look Like Plants:
look in rock pools and around timber breakwaters.

PURSE SPONGE

DAISY ANEMONE

JELLY-FISH

Fish

SAND EEL

LESSER WEAVER

15 SPINED STICKLEBACK

Animal In Armour

HERMIT CRAB

PRAWN

Seashore Worms:
found in the sand.

SCALE WORM

LUGWORM

Birds

HERRING GULL

KITTIWAKE

SANDWICH TERN

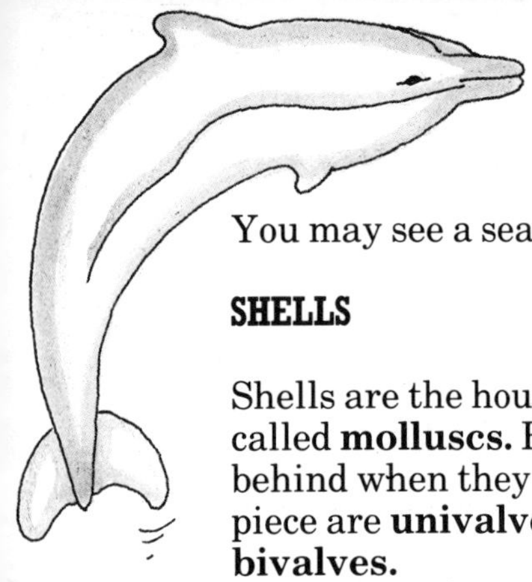

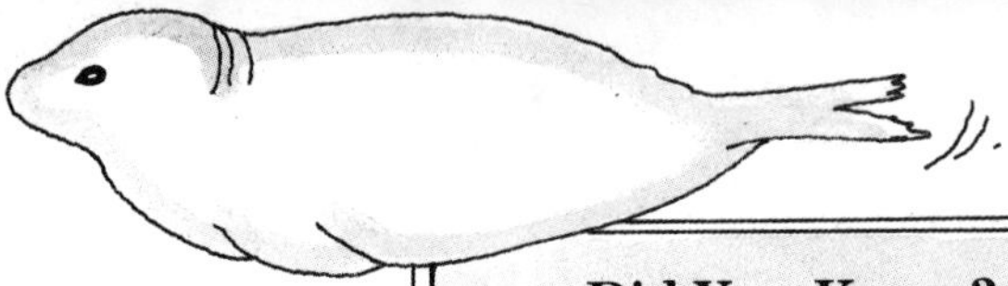

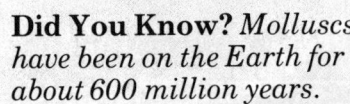

You may see a seal or a dolphin.

SHELLS

Shells are the houses of creatures called **molluscs.** Empty shells are left behind when they die. Shells in one piece are **univalves;** in two pieces – **bivalves.**

COCKLE

MUSCLE

SCALLOP

RAZOR

WHELK

PERIWINKLE

LIMPET

Did You Know? *Molluscs have been on the Earth for about 600 million years.*

Did You Know? *There are 800 species of mollusc in Britain. About 600 live in the sea.*

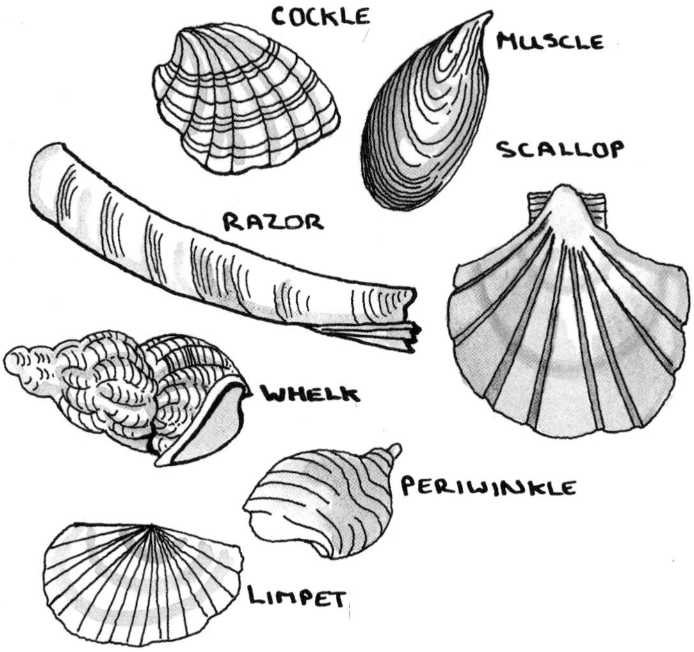

Collecting Shells . . . Tips:

★ Many shells will be damaged. Be patient and you will find good ones.
★ A small sieve is useful for uncovering tiny shells.
★ Put them in plastic bags or a box with cotton-wool.
★ Wash them in warm, soapy water. A teaspoon of bleach in cold water will remove stains.
★ Rinse them in cold water. Let them dry on a paper towel.
★ Rub on a little oil to make them shine.

You Can Use Shells To:

1. Decorate a hair comb; a belt; sunglasses; a note-pad: work out your pattern. Use quick-drying glue – and stick on your shells.

2. Make a necklace, bracelet or earrings: paint the shells gold, silver or in bright colours. Make a hole by gently tapping a needle with something heavy. Work the needle through the hole to make it bigger. Thread them onto strong sewing thread; or sew them onto ribbon.

3. Make a Shell Animal!

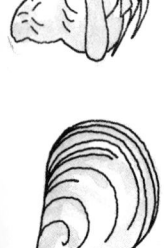

BE A BEACHCOMBER!

You never know what you may find on the beach. Look out for:

* **Pretty pebbles** * **Fossils, especially ammonites** * **Coins** * **Pieces of wood worn smooth by the sea** * **Interesting bottles**

Before you go off to the seaside or out and about – you want to know what the weather is going to be. This is how you can be ...

WEATHERPROOF

  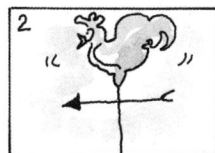   

BEAUFORT FORCE	TYPE OF WIND	EFFECTS TO LOOK FOR	SPEED IN MPH
0	CALM	Smoke rises vertically	0
1	LIGHT AIR	Smoke drifts	1-3
2	LIGHT BREEZE	Wind felt on face; leaves rustle; weather vane moves	4-7
3	GENTLE BREEZE	Leaves and small twigs move; flags extended	8-12
4	MODERATE BREEZE	Dust and loose paper blow about; small branches move	13-18
5	FRESH BREEZE	Small trees sway; wavelets form on water	19-24
6	STRONG BREEZE	Large branches sway; umbrellas used with difficulty; telegraph wires whistle	24-31
7	MODERATE GALE	Whole trees sway; hard to walk into the wind	32-38
8	GALE	Twigs break off trees; very hard to walk into the wind	39-46
9	STRONG GALE	Chimney pots and slates blown off	47-54
10	STORM	Trees uprooted; serious damage to buildings	55-63
11	VIOLENT STORM	Rarely occures inland; causes widespread damage	64-72
12	HURRICANE	Disastrous results	73

OBSTACLE LEAPFROG
As many players as possible.

To see who is *'frog'*, use this counting out rhyme:
> *Hibble, hobble, black bobble,*
> *Hibble hobble out,*
> *Turn the dirty dish cloth*
> *In-side-out!*

Then – the first person to leap over the *'frog'* places an object – a scarf; a book etc. – on the frog's back.

The other players have to leap over the object as well as the *'frog's'* back without knocking the object off! If they do, they become *'frog'*.

Add more and more objects to leap over.

What do you give a sea-sick elephant?

Plenty of room!

Postman Pat's PUZZLE PAGE

Can you find your way to the centre of the maze and help Postman Pat and Jess get the van keys back from the hen who has stolen them?

START

Postman Pat can't read the message on this card – can you help him?

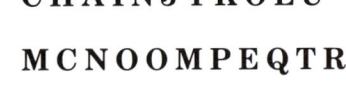

CHAINJYKOLU

MCNOOMPEQTRO

SMTYUPVAWRXTYYZOAN

BSCADTEUFRGDHAIYJMK

RLSMGNROOPGQGRISNTS

Postman Pat knows these letters come from different countries – but he doesn't know which ones. **Add a letter to the beginning and end . . . and see if you can find the country.**

RANC	REEC	PAI	APA	RA	OLAN

Would you like to be able to draw a cat like Jess?

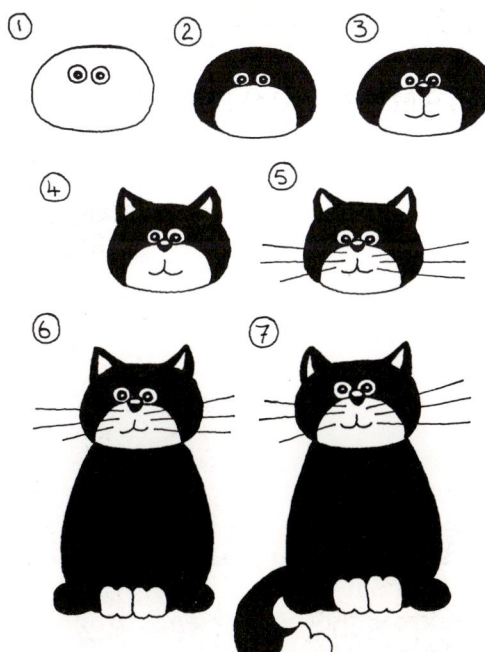

Answers:

Did You Find The Keys?

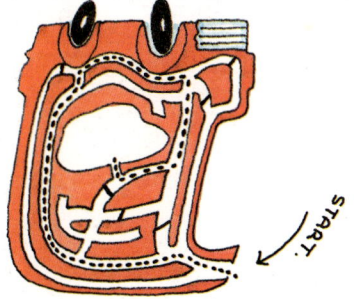

Secret Message:

SATURDAY MRS GROGGINS
CAN YOU COME TO MY PARTY ON

Cross out the 2nd letter, then every other letter to crack the code.

Which Country?

FRANCE, GREECE, SPAIN,
JAPAN, IRAQ, POLAND

RAINY DAYS

THIS IS YOUR LIFE!

Lots of things happen to you every day! Some of them are important to you, some of them are not. Before you forget too many things – why don't you make a **Life Chart**?

You Need: A long piece of paper (or tape two or three together); a ruler; pencil; coloured pens.

How To Make Your Life Chart:

1. Draw a line, lengthwise, across the middle of the paper. Then divide the line with a mark for each year of your life, plus an extra mark for next year. Going from left to right, write in the year by each mark.

2. Then in each year, write and draw in (above and below the line) all the important things that you can remember. Then ask members of your family what they can remember about you!

Here are some questions to jog your memory . . .

*When is your birthday?
If you have a younger brother or sister, when were they born?
What was your favourite toy?
What was the first thing you remember?
When was your first bike ride?
When could you read a book all on your own?*

*When did you meet your best friend?
What was the worst thing you've done?
When did you get a good/ bad school report?
When did the dog chew up your favourite teddy?*

You can always add on extra sheets of paper if you need more room.

If several of you are making **LIFE CHARTS** it will be interesting to compare what they remember, and what was important to them.

TIN FLIP (1 or more players)

You Need:

2 tins for each player with the top completely removed; a ball small enough to be covered by the tin; or – 1 ball and 2 tins and you take it in turns.

How to Play:

The aim is to hit the ball with one tin and trap it with the other tin – then flip and trap it back again.
How fast can you flip and trap?
How long can you do it before you miss the ball?
See who can flip and trap longest – and quickest?

IN ORDER
(1 or more players)

You Need: 2 dice – and patience!

How To Play:

You have to roll the dice so that **both** dice have the **SAME** number showing AND you have to try and throw them so that the two dice add up from **2 to 12** in numerical sequence!

As soon as you throw wrongly, the dice go to the next player – or start again if you are playing on your own.

COTTON-REEL RACER

To Make Your Reel-Racer You Will Need:

an empty cotton-reel
a small chunk of soap
a wide rubber band a little shorter than the reel
4 or 5 used wooden match-sticks
scissors

How To Make Your Reel-Racer:

1. Cut a circle of soap a little smaller than the top of the reel. Make it about 1cm thick. (You may need to get some help.) Make a hole with the sharp point of the scissors in the middle of the soap. Then rub the groove across the middle with a match-stick.

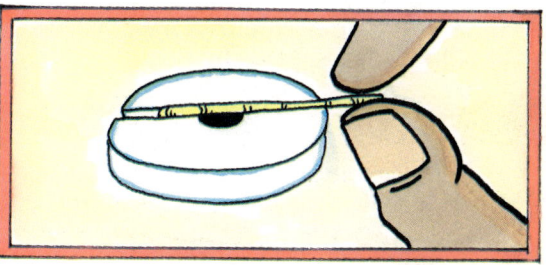

2. Push the rubber band through the hole in the middle of the cotton-reel.

3. Use a short piece of match-stick to keep the rubber band in place, as shown in the picture.

SEE WHAT'S ON THE NEXT PAGE!

4. Push the other end of the rubber band through the hole in the middle of the soap circle. You must have the groove facing out.

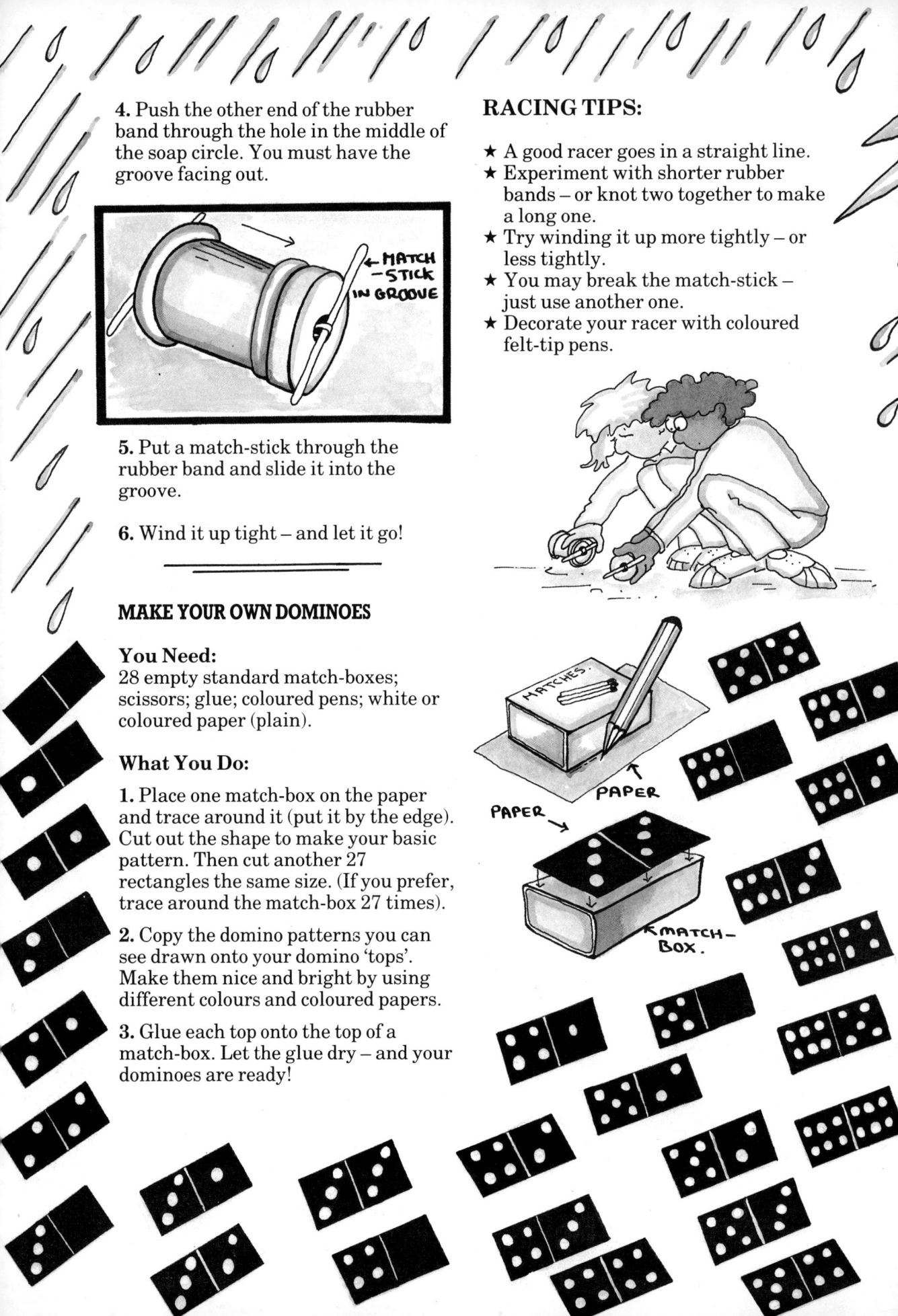

← MATCH
-STICK
IN GROOVE

5. Put a match-stick through the rubber band and slide it into the groove.

6. Wind it up tight – and let it go!

MAKE YOUR OWN DOMINOES

You Need:
28 empty standard match-boxes; scissors; glue; coloured pens; white or coloured paper (plain).

What You Do:

1. Place one match-box on the paper and trace around it (put it by the edge). Cut out the shape to make your basic pattern. Then cut another 27 rectangles the same size. (If you prefer, trace around the match-box 27 times).

2. Copy the domino patterns you can see drawn onto your domino 'tops'. Make them nice and bright by using different colours and coloured papers.

3. Glue each top onto the top of a match-box. Let the glue dry – and your dominoes are ready!

RACING TIPS:

★ A good racer goes in a straight line.
★ Experiment with shorter rubber bands – or knot two together to make a long one.
★ Try winding it up more tightly – or less tightly.
★ You may break the match-stick – just use another one.
★ Decorate your racer with coloured felt-tip pens.

MATCHES

PAPER

PAPER →

←MATCH-
BOX.

There are many domino games you
can play – here is one:

DOUBLES (2 or more players)

How To Play:

1. The first player is chosen by lot. This
is done by all the players picking a
domino 'blind'. Whowever has the most
pips – starts.

2. Shuffle the dominoes face
downwards. When there are 2, 3 or 4
players, each player draws seven
dominoes. When there are 5 players,
they draw 5 dominoes. The remaining
dominoes form the **'boneyard',** the
central extra pool.

3. The first player plays a double by
putting it in the middle of the table. If
he hasn't got a double, he must draw
from the boneyard until he gets one.

4. The next player must match one end
of the first player's double. If he can't,
he must draw from the boneyard until
he can.

5. The next player must match the
other end of the first player's double,
and draw from the boneyard if he needs
to.

6. The second and third
dominoes must now be
matched with their doubles.
If the players do not have the right
dominoes in their hand, then they must
take from the boneyard. When there
are no more domnoes in the boneyard,
the player must 'pass'.

At all times the pattern of the line
must be: **double - matching domino –
double – matching domino –
double.** Doubles must alternate with
two figure dominoes.
The first player to go out by getting rid
of all his dominoes – is the winner.

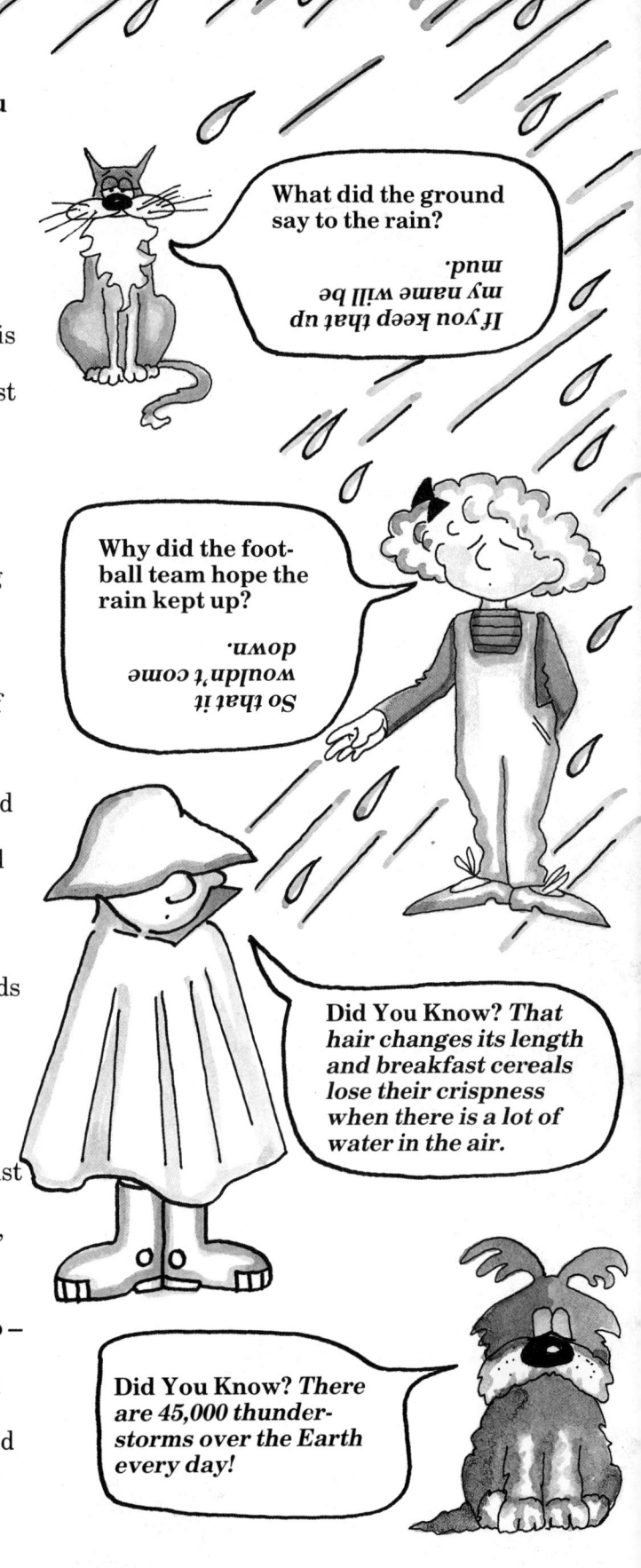

What did the ground
say to the rain?

*If you keep that up
my name will be
mud.*

Why did the foot-
ball team hope the
rain kept up?

*So that it
wouldn't come
down.*

Did You Know? *That
hair changes its length
and breakfast cereals
lose their crispness
when there is a lot of
water in the air.*

Did You Know? *There
are 45,000 thunder-
storms over the Earth
every day!*

DRESSING UP   Would you like to be a **ROBOT**?

You Need:

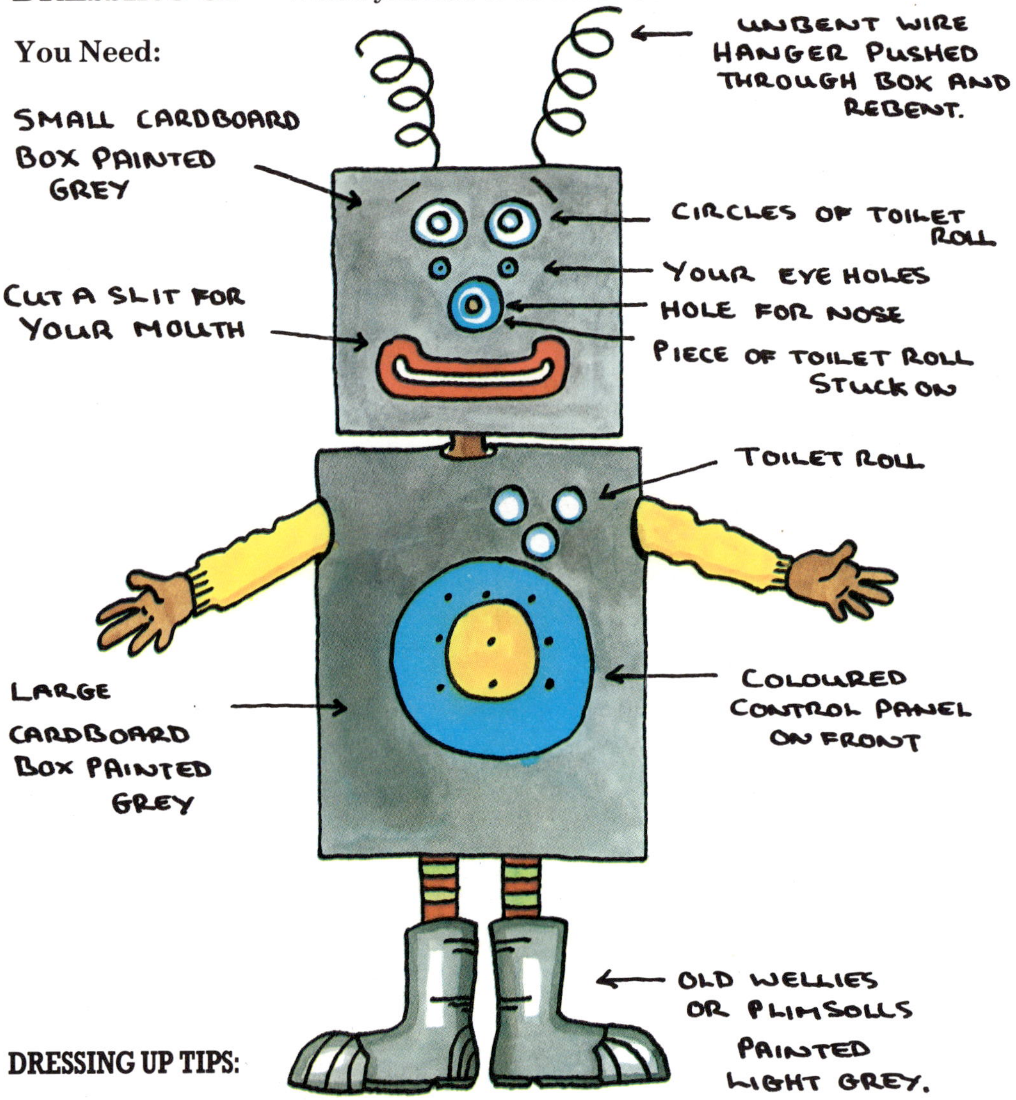

SMALL CARDBOARD BOX PAINTED GREY

CUT A SLIT FOR YOUR MOUTH

LARGE CARDBOARD BOX PAINTED GREY

UNBENT WIRE HANGER PUSHED THROUGH BOX AND REBENT.

CIRCLES OF TOILET ROLL

YOUR EYE HOLES

HOLE FOR NOSE

PIECE OF TOILET ROLL STUCK ON

TOILET ROLL

COLOURED CONTROL PANEL ON FRONT

OLD WELLIES OR PLIMSOLLS PAINTED LIGHT GREY.

DRESSING UP TIPS:

To Change Your Shape:

Tie cushions in the right places! On your back – for a hunched back:

around your tummy to look fat!

Or . . . a **CLOWN?**

FLOWER

OLD FELT HAT

PIECES OF WOOL TAPED INSIDE THE HAT.

MAKE UP FACE

BRACES

PLASTIC WATERING CAN

TEE-SHIRT

PAIR OF YOUR FATHERS OLD TROUSERS

CIRCLES OF COLOURED FELT SEWN ON

WHITE SOCKS WITH CIRCLES

OLD PLIMSOLLS WITH PAINT.

Beards and Moustaches:

Fold a piece of cardboard in half. Draw on it the shape you want for your beard or moustache (make sure it's big enough to fit). Cut it out. Unfold it. Stick on pieces of black or brown or ginger wool. Use **tape** to stick them to you.

COVER SHAPE WITH WOOL

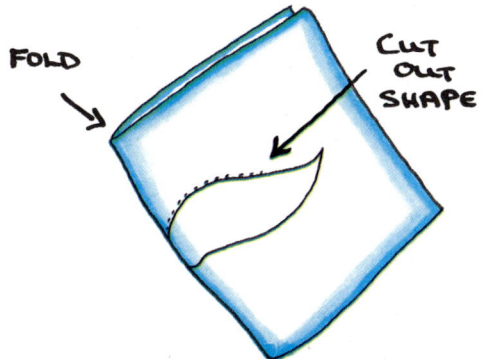

FOLD

CUT OUT SHAPE

Teeth:

NEVER PUT GLUE IN YOUR MOUTH!

To Black-out Teeth: use double-sided tape to stick a small piece of black paper to the tooth or teeth.
For Dracula Teeth: roll a piece of paper into a cone. Tape it together. Cut the end straight and fix it over your tooth.

Masks:

Paint your 'face' on one side of a paper bag. Cut out holes for your nose, eyes and mouth. You can also make a half-mask ending at your nose.

Banners and Spears:

Paint an old broom handle.
Spear: cut out the end from a piece of card. Paint it grey or silver and glue it to one end of the broom.

CARD

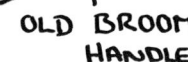

OLD BROOM HANDLE

Banner: paint your design on an old piece of plain material. Cut it out on a circle or a square or with pointed edges. Sew ribbon to the top and bottom of one side and then tie it to the top of your broom handle.

Swords and Shields:

Sword: draw the shape of the blade and handle on stiff card. Cut it out. Paint the blade silver or grey, and the handle GOLD!

Shield: draw the shape you want on card. Cut it out. Draw a design on it and paint it. Staple a loop of card on the back large enough for you to put your hand through.

If you enjoy dressing up – why don't you start a **DRESSING UP BOX?**

Useful things to put in it:

belts	pieces of bright
scarves	material
shawls	wire
hats	paper clips
old curtains	paper plates

pyjamas	empty toilet
old shoes	rolls
kitchen foil	old make up
sunglasses	cans of spray
plasticine	paint

Why don't you have a party on a theme – **THE CIRCUS, OUTER SPACE, SPIES?**

Everyone has to dress up – and all the games and the food can fit your theme too!

THE TREE WITH THE DIFFICULT NAME

Many, many years ago, hard times came to Africa. For many seasons the rains didn't fall and the animals had to move from place to place in their search for food.

At last, after they had wandered a great distance, they came to a huge tree covered with the most delicious-looking fruit. There was only one problem. None of the animals knew the name of the tree, but they all knew that it was **never** safe to eat the fruit of a tree unless the name of the tree was known.

A bird flying past did tell them something about the tree. It belonged to an old, old woman called Koko who lived a long way away. She would know the name of the tree, not just what sort of tree it was, but the name of that particular tree.

There was only one thing to do. One of them would have to go and find Koko and ask her the name of the tree. The tree bore so much fruit, that they were sure the old woman would be willing to share some of it with them and tell them the name of the tree.

The hare could travel quickly, and so the hare was chosen to go and find the old woman. He had to go down by the river, and after going a long way, he at last found the old woman called Koko.

The hare went up to her and said: 'Grandmother Koko, we animals have travelled far in search of food and we are all dying of hunger. Please may we eat some of the fruit that grows on your tree? Please will you tell me the name of the tree?'

'Of course you can eat from my tree' said Koko. 'All you have to do is stand underneath it and say its name – **UWUNGELEMA.**'

'What a difficult name! **U-WUNG-GELEMA!**' repeated the hare. 'Thank you, thank you Grandmother Koko.'

The hare raced back as fast as he could to the other animals repeating to himself as he ran **'U-WUNG-GELEMA. U-WUNG-GELEMA.'** But the hare was running so fast that he wasn't looking where he was going, and suddenly he tripped over a root in the path, and fell and banged his head. The hare was quite dazed by his bump on the head, and, to his horror, he couldn't remember the name of the tree.

'OO...WU...' he knew the name sounded something like that and the hare was sure that when he got back to the other animals, he would remember it.

But when he got back to the other animals waiting by the tree all he could say when they asked him for the name the old woman Koko had given him was:

'OO WU ... something like that.'

All the animals exclaimed: 'That's no good! We need to have the whole name of the tree!' So the animals decided to send TWO messengers, and the two big elands set off to find the old woman called Koko.

The elands raced down the path by the river until they came to the old woman called Koko. They asked her the same question as the hare had done, and she gave them the same answer. This time, however, she added something else to her answer:

'Whatever you do, brave elands, do not look behind you on your way back to the other animals.'

The elands thanked her for her help and for her advice, and dashed off back to the other animals. But as they raced along they kept hearing strange noises in the bush behind them as though some strange animal was following them – and one of the elands looked back.

To their horror, when they reached the other animals, they had both **FORGOTTEN** the name of the tree.

'Well' said the animals, 'We have now sent three fast messengers to find out the name of the tree, and no-one has been able to remember it by the time they have returned to us. This time, somebody will have to go to the old woman Koko by another route.'

So the animals decided that they would have to reach her by the river, and the Mongoose said he would take a canoe and try and get the name of the tree.

So the Mongoose padded down the river to Koko, and she gave him the same answer.

'U-WUNG-GELEMA!' the Mongoose repeated carefully. 'Thank you! Thank you for giving us the name again.'

As he was leaving, Koko said one more thing to the Mongoose. 'When you are on your way back to the other animals in your canoe, you must not eat any of the food, or drink any of the water that you have brought with you.'

The return journey was not so easy for the Mongoose, and he had to paddle against the strong current all the way. He felt so tired, and so faint, and so hungry from his efforts that he ate a small mouthful of the food he had brought with him. And when he got back to the other animals – he had forgotten the name of the tree!

The other animals were furious with him. They called him names but it didn't alter the fact: he had forgotten the name.

The Lion then decided that as he was king, that he had better go himself. Well, the Lion went to see Koko, and she gave him the name of the tree, and he repeated it to himself all the way back so that he would not forget it.

'UWUNGELEMA! UWUNGELE-MA! UWUNGELEMA!' he growled over and over. He repeated it so often that, after a while, the word sounded to him like nonsense, and so when he got back to the other animals, he was just as bad as the Hare.

All he could say was:

'It begins with Oooo and then goes on with a Woo . . . .'

Then the big Buffalo went; then the little gazelles raced off; and one by one **all** the animals, except the Tortoise, had been to Koko to get the name of the tree, and not one of them could remember it by the time they returned.

'Let Me Go' said the Tortoise.

At first the other animals shook their heads. How could the Tortoise, who was the slowest animal of all, hope to remember the name of the tree. Then they decided that as everyone of

them had tried and failed, there was no harm in letting the Tortoise see what he could do.

So the Tortoise set off, going very, very slow, but very, very steadily on his short little legs, and at last he reached the old woman Koko.

Please will you tell me the name of the tree,' asked the Tortoise. 'All the animals are starving, and not one of them was able to remember the name by the time they returned to us.'

'That is very sad' said Koko. 'Perhaps they all went too fast. Now you must go back very slowly.'

'I always go very slowly,' said the Tortoise. 'But I am afraid that because I can only go slowly I will have forgotten the name by the time I get back. It will take me such a long time to make the journey!'

'I have an idea,' said Koko. 'I will give you a little bell, and as you go along, the little bell will ring, and the sound of its bell as it rings will sound to you just like U-WUNG-GELEMA!' So Koko brought the tortoise a little bell and tied it around his neck.

And it happened just as the old woman Koko had said. As the Tortoise walked, oh so slowly, along the path back to the other animals, the little bell rang, and each time it rang, the bell said 'U-WUNG-GELEMA' to the Tortoise.

It took the Tortoise a very long time to make his way back, and he began to feel very tired. Just as he thought he was not going to make it back, he saw the other animals, grouped under the tree, waiting for his return.

The Tortoise was so tired that he could only just shout out 'U-WUNG-GELEMA!', but the other animals heard.

Then all the animals at the top of their voices shouted 'U-WUNG-GELEMA', and the fruit from the tree rained down on them.

They all had a wonderful feast on the lovely ripe fruit, and then all the animals slept until late the next morning. When they awoke, all the animals cried out:

'Mr. Tortoise, you will be our Chief. You were the only one who was able to remember the name of the tree, and you saved us all from starving.'

FLYING HIGH

A NEWSPAPER KITE

You can even fly it in the rain!

You Need:
A large newspaper (ask your
newsagent to keep an old copy of the
Times, Guardian or one of that size).
Tape; a button; sewing thread;
4 drinking straws;
A reel of string;
Ruler; pencil; scissors.

How To Make Your Kite:

1. Take a double page from the
newspaper. Fold it in half, at its fold,
and press your thumb along the edge to
make a sharp crease. With a blunt
knife carefully slit down the crease to
give 2 pages.

2. Fold both pages in half again,
horizontally. Make another sharp
crease on each, and slit down to give 4
separate sheets.

3. Fold all 4 pieces in half, horizontally,
to make 4 tent-shaped pieces.
Take 2 of these tents and fold them in
half, lengthwise, and then in half
again. Then open them out. The
creases will look like the illustration
(3).

4. On these two tents draw 2 lines, as
shown, and then cut away the shaded
areas. This will leave you with 2
diamond shapes **(a),** creased through
the centre, which will become the
wings and keel of the kite.

5. Take one of the uncut sheets, and lay
it flat **(b).** This will be the main body of
the kite.

Place the edges of the 2 diamonds **(a)**
against the 2 longest edges of **(b).** Hold
them in position with weights (books).
Then join the edges together with tape.

6. Fold out each diamond flat to make the wings and keels. Weight the kite flat and then put a piece of tape across the total width of the kite.

7. To Make The Kite Sticks: take another spread from the newspaper. Crease and cut it in half, as before. Take one of the sheets, crease, and cut it in half.

8. Take a drinking straw to the bottom left-hand corner of each sheet. Tightly roll it, diagonally, to the opposite corner of the sheet. Tape the sticks firmly together.

Fold the stick ends down to make one stick 60cm long, and two 40cm long. Cut the ends off.

9. Tape the 40cm spine sticks to the kite **(points c)**, leaving a little over the edge. The tail towing line will be tied to them.

10. Carefully unstick the tape in the middle, where the keels are stuck down. Cut through it at point them. Fold the keels upwards.

11. Turn the kite over. Tape the long stick from wing to tip to wing tip. Tie 80cm of thread to the overlapping spines. Then measure the thread up to the centre of the stick and tie it in a loop.

12. To Make The Tail: fold the last tent in half. Crease and cut. Fold each half in half, then in half again, and in half again. Press the creases. Cut at the creases to give you 16 strips.

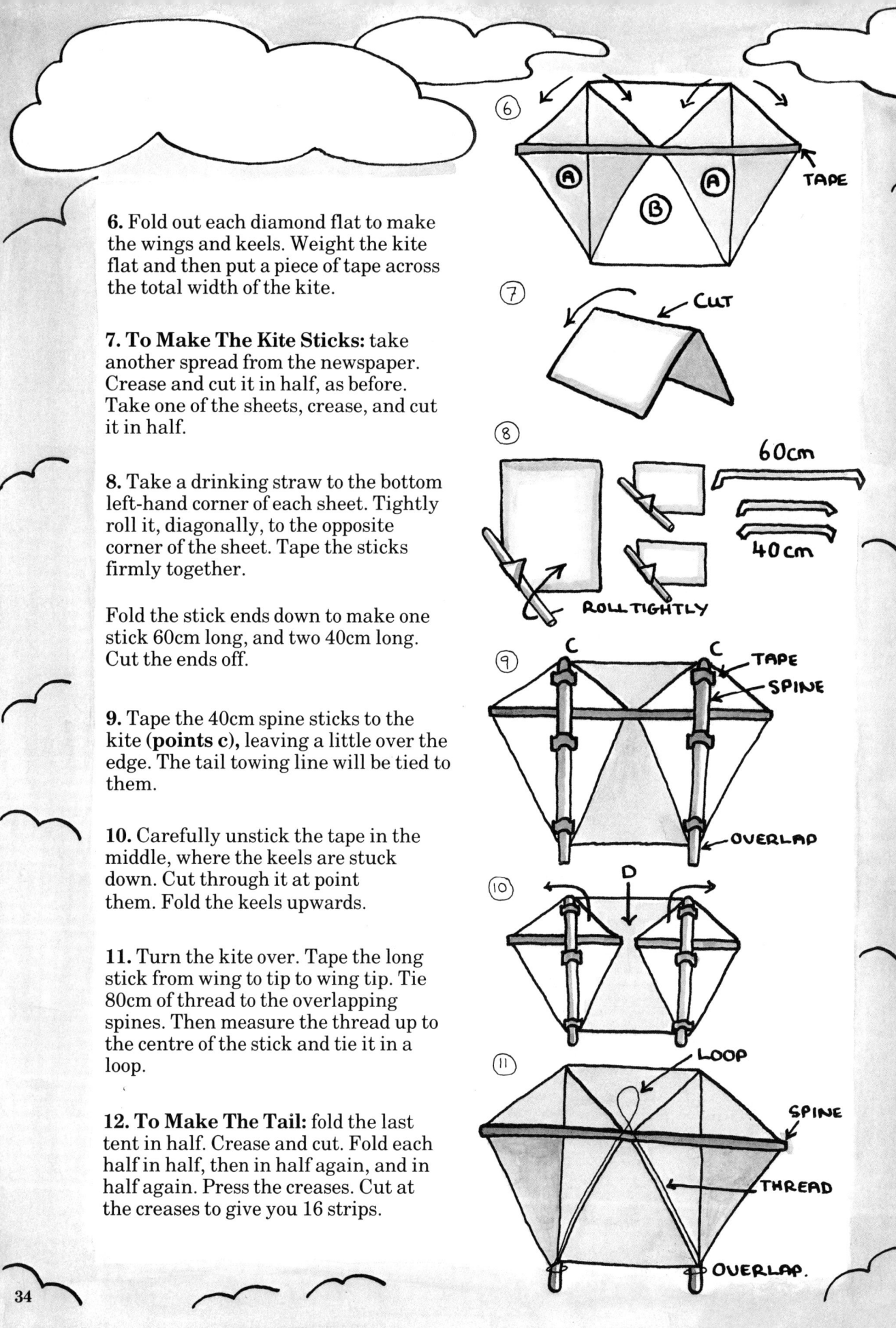

34

Measure a metre of thread. Take 8 strips and tie them round the middle with the end of the thread. Tie the other 8 round the middle – half way up the thread.

13. Thread the other end of the metre onto a needle and push it through the last straw. Push the needle and thread through the button, and knot it firmly. Tape the straw to the tail loop.

14. Measure another metre of thread. Make a small hole in the top of each keel. Thread the cotton through and knot it to keep it attached. Measure of the half-way point of the thread and tie a loop for towing. Tie the end of the reel of string firmly to the towing loop – and your kite is **READY!**

If you follow these instructions slowly and carefully – you will find your kite easy to make. If you get stuck – ask for some help. It is made of paper – so transport it carefully.

FLYING TIPS:

★ **NEVER** fly your kite near electricity wires.
★ The best places to fly are on rolling hills, or flat ground.
★ Stand with your back to the wind to launch it. Hold the kite up to the wind with one hand, and hold the towing line with the other.
★ As your kite rises, let the line tug gently through your fingers.
★ If your kite drops pull it evenly towards you.
★ Never run with your kite.
★ If you let the line run through your fingers, the kite will fall away from you and sink. Walk away from it pulling the line in.

★ If it becomes skittish, walk slowly towards it, letting the line out slowly.
★ Get to know the feel of your kite. You may need more strips on the tail to balance it.

USEFUL ADDRESSES:
**British Kite Fliers Assocation
P.O. Box, 35,
Hemel Hempstead,
Herts.**

**The Kite Society,
31 Grange Road,
Ilford,
Surrey.**

TOAD'S ROAD GAME

For 2 or more players

You will need: a dice, a shaker and different coloured counters or buttons for each player.

4 Take short cut to 13

9 Avoid bends by taking short cut A-I

16 Give lift to Chief Weasel. Go on to 25.

11 PUNCTURE. Throw 4, 5 or 6 to get going again.

18 Sheep crossing road. Miss a turn.

B Level crossing shu Miss a turn.

26 Take humpback bridge fast but safely. Go to 32.

22 Take a short cut A-F.

20 Fall in ditch, cornering too fast. Miss a turn.

24 Spare wheel drops off. Go back to 12 for replacement.

27 Take wrong turning straight into river. Miss a turn.

H Drive slowly across ford. Throw 1, 3 or 5 to move.

34 Take a short cut A-E.

41 Stopped by policeman for speeding round bend. Miss a turn.

45 Straight stretch of road. Speed straight on to 57.

48 Take wrong turning, back to 35.

50 Put on speed to avoid following police car. Go to 59.

36

99 Car slows up on hill. Throw 2, 4 or 6 to keep moving.

101 Speed downhill to Toad Hall and home.

100 101 102 103 104 99 98 97 96 94 95

93 93 Pick up two stoats and hurry them straight to 98.

92

HOME

90 Decide to look in on Ratty again. Miss a turn.

86 Race train to level crossing. Go to 92.

91 Level crossing shut for train. Miss a turn.

91 90 89 88 87 86 85 84

G F E D C B A

81 Give lift to Mole who is in a hurry to get home to Ratty. Go straight to 89.

83

78 79 80 81 82

77 76 75 74 73

77 Slow down to watch Ratty rowing. Throw 1, 3 or 5 to get going.

D C B A

C Pigs in the road. Miss a turn.

73 You realise you are near Ratty's house. Hurry to visit him. Go straight to F.

72

68 Take wrong turning. Go back to 56.

71 70 69 68 67 66 65 64

66 Take short cut A-D.

63

70 Held up by cows going to farm for milking. Miss a turn.

C B A

62

61

53 54 55 56 57 58 59 60

55 Take a short cut to 69.

58 Stopped by policeman for speeding. Throw 5 or 6 to get started.

LET'S HAVE A PICNIC

The most important thing to remember when you are getting your picnic together is that – **you are going to have to carry it!**

MOUTH-WATERING SANDWICHES

Sandwich-Making Tips:

★ Don't make the filling too runny.
★ Don't fill it too full so that the filling oozes out everywhere.
★ Take the butter out of the fridge a little before you make them so it is soft and easy to spread.
★ Wrap them in silver-foil or cling-film to keep them fresh.

Make your sandwiches with fillings you haven't tried before like:

Banana and peanut butter
Tuna and gherkins
Cream cheese, raisins
and lettuce
Chicken and mayonnaise
Cheese and marmite
Cold Bacon and tomato

Try and pack your picnic in a bag or knapsack you can carry over your shoulder.

To make your picnic extra special, put in a treat for yourself – AND treats to share! Always try and put in a bar of chocolate.

ORANGE FIZZ

Drink is essential on a picnic.
You Need: a plastic bottle (clean) with a tight screw top.

To Make Orange Fizz You Need:
a small can of frozen, concentrated orange juice, thawed
300ml lemonade
½ an orange

Mix the orange juice and lemonade in a jug. Slice the orange and then cut it into small pieces (to go in the top of the bottle and out again!). Stir it all up. Pour you **Orange Fizz** into your drinking bottle. Screw the top on tightly – to keep your drink in – and to keep it fizzy.

How do you make toast in the jungle?

Under a gorilla.

What's yellow and stupid?

Thick custard.

How do you make a sausage roll?

Push it.

STICK-JAW TOFFEE

You Need: 175 grammes of butter
200 gramme tin
condensed milk
225 grammes soft
brown sugar
225 grammes golden
syrup

What You Do:

1. Rub a tin, about 28x18cms with a little piece of butter to grease it.

2. Melt the butter in a large saucepan.

3. Add the sugar and syrup. Heat it gently to dissolve the sugar. Stir it. When it boils add the condensed milk.

4. Boil for about 20 minutes. Keep stirring with a wooden spoon. It will gradually thicken and go mid-brown in colour.

5. Drop a small amount into a saucer of cold water. If it forms a soft round ball, it is ready.

6. Pour your toffee into the greased tin. Let it get cold – then break it into pieces.

Other picnic ingredients:

sausage rolls
a tomato
a hard-boiled egg
an apple
a bag of crisps
a piece of cake
a bag for rubbish
a serviette

Wrap the food up in separate packages.
YUM YUM!

ROUND SOFT TOFFEE BALL

Did You Know? *Peanuts are used in the manufacture of gunpowder.*

Did You Know? *Primitive man used butter as a body ointment.*

DID I EVER TELL YOU . . .
About Being Banned for
Life from the Boating Pool?   by Iris Grender

Soon after my brother Francis had his eighth birthday we went to stay with our friends in Hastings. We always liked that as it was better than an ordinary holiday by the sea. They lived at the sea and we could come and go as we pleased. They were a small family, just Auntie Lily and two boys called Peter and David. David was just a little older than Francis, and Peter was just a little younger than me. We always had a nice time together. Sometimes we played on the beach and sometimes we played in the park. It was a marvellous park. It had everything in it and the best thing of all was the boating pool. We didn't have one like it at home.

David and Peter went to the boating pool very often. They liked it as much as swimming in the sea. It didn't cost much. There was a man in charge who took the money and showed you which boat you could have. Then you rowed about on the pool just like real sailors. After half an hour the boatman would put a loudspeaker to his mouth and call

your number, saying, 'Come in, number three' – or number fourteen or whatever your number was. Then you knew it was time to stop and take you boat back.

When we were staying in Hastings we never wasted our money on sweets or ice creams. We always needed every penny we could find for the boating pool. We often rowed up and down and then went home to ask if we could have the money for another boat. Sometimes we had two boats and once we had a boat each and that was the best of all, but that was the last time we ever went there.

When we had two boats, David and Peter taught us to play pirates. You had to get into your boat and row very fast after your friends. When you caught them, you had to grab the rope from their boat and try to pull them along. Sometimes all three of us would capture David. He would sit in his boat yelling angrily as we captured him. Once he lost his oars in the water and the boatman came along the bank and

shouted at us to stop before he fell in. That time we did stop.

The next time we had two boats, we played pirates and caught some children we had never seen before. Peter got really excited and climbed into their boat, telling them that they were captured and that he was the captain now. When they took their boat back, they complained to the boat keeper.

When we took our boats back, we all stood in a row and hung our heads as the boat keeper told us what he thought about our unruly behaviour.

'Don't ever do that again,' he said, 'or you won't be able to hire another boat.'

Unfortunately children sometimes forget stern warnings, especially when they are enjoying themselves.

The next morning our mothers gave us enough money for a boat each. It was thrilling because we could all be captains and row ourselves about without taking turns. David captured Francis and let him go again. Then Peter nearly captured me. Francis captured a man rowing his little boy around the pool. That was quite the wrong thing to do. The boat keeper leaped into his boat and rowed out to us. To escape, we rowed in all directions. It was as though the boat keeper had suddenly joined in our game of pirates.

'Abandon your boats,' yelled David.

With that he rowed his boat to the side, leaped out and ran across the park. The three of us did the same, leaving four boats bobbing about on the pool. We didn't stop until we arrived home quite out of breath and panting.

The next time we went to the park to hire a boat, of course the boat keeper said no. 'Don't ever come here again!' he said. 'You're all banned for life. You look old enough to know better,' he told David and Francis.

As we walked home Francis said, 'That's the trouble with being eight. Everyone expects you to be really grown-up. I wish I was only seven again.'

And that's how we all came to be banned for life from the boating pool.

KEEP YOUR EYES OPEN!

Look around you and count to five. Then shut your eyes. Try to remember everything you have seen. Then open them – and see how many things you forgot and how many things you missed seeing altogether!

If you keep your eyes open you will be amazed at all the things you can find!

WHAT'S IN A HEDGE?

Some hedges – the ones along an old parish boudary – are hundreds of years old. Some were planted yesterday. If a hedge has been there a long time, many birds will have visited it and dropped seeds from a wide variety of trees and shrubs.

Why don't you and a couple of friends look at a hedge through the holidays? How many different shrubs and plants can you see? (They will have different-shaped leaves.)

How many different plants, insects, birds and animals can you find?

A hedge will contain different things at different times of the year.

How Old Is Your Hedge?

If you live in an old town or village and you think your hedge may be hundreds of years old – you can work out its age.

1. Mark the hedge into three 30 metre sections.

2. Count the number of different shrubs in each section.

3. Take the average for the three sections. Multiply the average by 110 – and you will have the age of your hedge!

In the spring and summer look out for:

COW PARSLEY

HAWTHORN

HEDGE SPARROW

YELLOWHAMMER

GREEN VEINED WHITE BUTTERFLY

CUCKOO SPIT

DOG ROSE

MEADOW BARLEY

CAPSID BUG

MARBLE GALLS

CATERPILLARS

CHRYSALIS

LIME STONE

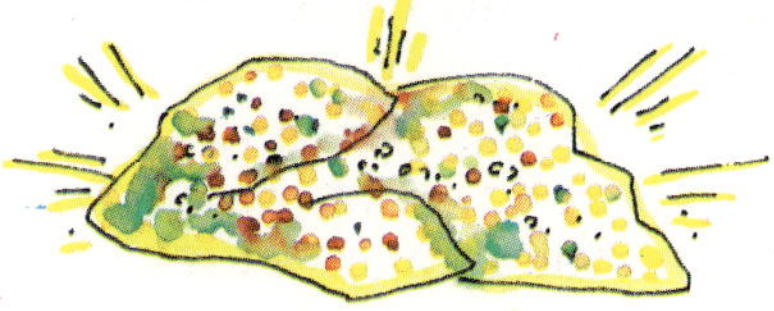

SAND STONE

TOUGH GRANITE

MARBLE

BASALT

POLISHED STONE

BANK

SLATE

ROCKS AND MINERAL

Almost all the earth is made of rocks and minerals. Look closely at the buildings near you, especially churches, and see if you can find:

Limestone: often pale yellow in colour. Look closely. You may find fossil shells in it.

Sandstone: made from sparkly sand-grains.

Tough granite: reddish if it comes from the North; white or grey if it comes from Cornwall. It is made from a mass of crystals of different colours and shapes.

Marble: formed from limestone, is often used in churches and banks.

Basalt: formed from cooled lava, may have been used to make the pavement and kerb because it is very strong.

Polished stone: often used on the front of banks.

Slate: formed from shale – and used for roofing tiles.

TRACKS AND TRAILS

You may not see them but many
animals live near you.

Look for their tracks:
★ In soft mud.
★ By streams and ditches.
★ In hard snow.
★ Along paths – especially those of
  deer, badgers and rabbits. In ditches
  and under hedges – mainly rats and
  weasels.
★ Cats and foxes – make their own
  trails.

RABBIT

St. BERNARD DOG

CAT

HEDGEHOG

FOX

SPARROW

RAT

HORSES HOOF

IN THE STREETS

When you walk down the High Street, have you ever **LOOKED UP?**

You may think the buildings are new because the shops are modern, but many of the buildings are old, and the tops of them have not been changed.

Look out for:
> **Unusual-shaped windows**
> **Inscriptions**
> **Carved dates**
> **Plaster and stone**
> **decorations**
> **Towers and turrets**
> **Old signs**
> **Plaques**

How many **unusual signs** are there around where you live? Have you ever wondered where they lead to or what they mean?

Have you ever noticed signs like:

MUTTON'S . . . Master-Butchers

or a chair outside a shop, with a sign on it saying:

FOR TIRED DOGS
(ie. tired feet!)

Also look out for:

Coats-of-Arms: you could try and find out what family they belong to and borrow a library book to find out what the patterns mean. Are any of them Royal coats-of-arms?

Letter-boxes: are they all the same shape? Are there any old ones near you? Do you know how old they are?

These are just a few ideas. The more you look, the more you will see!

ON YOUR BIKE

How good a bike rider are you?
Can you balance?
Can you steer round tricky corners?
Can you brake quickly without skidding?

Try some of these games and races – and find out!

BEFORE YOU START: Make sure you ride your bike where it is safe from cars. If you are in the street NEVER let a game or a race course cross the road!

IT'S ON YOUR HEAD!

You Need: an old book for each player.

The Game:

Each biker must balance the book on their head – and ride around without it falling off! Whoever keeps it balanced longest – wins!

You can also mark out a course to ride – and take it in turns, with the book on your head, to see who can ride it quickest – AND without dropping the book.

Did You Know? *That bicycles were built with sails – and also with blades for travelling on ice!*

Did You Know? *That track bikes have no brakes or gears.*

Did You Know? *That a man-powered vehicle is called a* **velocipede** *– and that the first known ancestor of the bicycle was built by the Frenchman Comte de Sivrac in 1791. It was peddled with the feet, like a scooter.*

Why did the motorist drive his car in reverse?

Because he knew the Highway Code backwards!

FOLLOW MY LEADER

Choose a leader.

Then:
The leader sets off and everyone has to follow in single file.

The leader rides the trickiest course she can to lose her followers. Every one has to follow her course **EXACTLY!** Any follower who comes off it, even by tiny amount, is **OUT.**

TORTOISE RACE

How To Race:
Mark your start and finish line. All the racers line up at the start. At the word 'Go' from the starter, the racers must pedal **as slowly as they can** to the finish. Whoever is **LAST** – wins.

You must keep moving. If you put your foot on the ground you are **OUT.**

TAG

You Need For Each Biker:
A piece of string about 4m long
A piece of waste paper.

What You Do:

Tie one end of the string either to the rear mudguard – or to the back frame of your bike.

Tie the paper to the other end. You want it to trail out behind you as you ride.

Set boundaries. Anyone who rides outside them is **OUT.**
Use a counting out rhyme to decide who is **IT.**

How To Play:

Everyone rides about and IT tries to catch the string of the bikers with a wheel or a foot. Once a biker is tagged, they are **IT.**

RIDICULOUS RIDDLES

What did the grape say when the elephant trod on it?

It just gave out a little wine . . .

What do you call a man who can sing and drink at the same time?

A pop singer.

What's black and white and bounces?

A rubber nun.

What do you call a man with an oil rig on his head?

Derek.

Why is there no such thing as a whole day?

Because every morning day breaks.

What's the best day for cooking eggs and bacon?

Fryday.

Diner: Waiter, waiter, there's a cockroach in my soup!
Waiter: That's unusual. It's usually a fly.